You Are In
Great Demand

This book will help you transition from being a person with great needs into a person who is greatly needed.

Robert L. Smith

Tulsa, Oklahoma

YOU ARE IN GREAT DEMAND
© 2005 by Robert L. Smith

Published by Insight Publishing Group
8801 S. Yale, Suite 410
Tulsa, OK 74137
918-493-1718

Unless otherwise noted, all Scripture quotations are taken from the Holy Bible: King James Version. Scripture quotations marked NKJV are taken from the *Holy Bible: The New King James Version*, © 1979, 1980, 1982 by Thomas Nelson, Inc., publishers.

ISBN 1-932503-50-1
1. Christian Life

Library of Congress catalog card number: 2004116630

Printed in the United States of America

DEDICATION

To Linda, my wife of twenty-five years, and our sons Cedric in Aurora, Colorado and Justin in Alexandria, Virginia.

CONTENTS

FOREWORD

As I read this book my spirit leaped inside for joy because I felt so needed and so important. This book tremendously blessed me. I truly know that this book is from the throne room of heaven, God speaking to His people encouraging them to know that they are in great demand. I thank God for Minister Smith allowing the Holy Spirit to flow through him for such a time as this to help all. This word will make an impact on millions.

Pastor W Irvin Jenkins, Sr.
Spartanburg, SC

ACKNOWLEDGMENT

I'm grateful for the inspiration and dedication of a couple of people who gave their time and energy to see this book published.

Linda Smith, Alexandria, VA
Kristy Hathorn, Jackson, MS

INTRODUCTION

The world is filled with people in trouble and despair. They are feverishly looking for solutions and something real. The demand for help increases daily. The poverty, divorce, and violence rates indicate that people are in need. The demand is great for both the impoverished and the prosperous. People want relief. Lasting relief is in the supreme reliever, God. He is in great demand. He's in great demand in lives of believers and non-believers. Is this demand too great for God?[1] No!

God helps people through people. As you are reading this book, God is helping you. God will help others through you. Others need God's help and you are one He can use to help them. There are others in circumstances tailor made for your kind of help. You were destined to be in demand. You may have evaluated yourself as being incapable of helping anyone. You know what it is like to be in need.[2] Therefore, you will not make light of their situation. You'll always have needs. But your needs will not always have you. You are more than capable of helping others.

It's not by chance that you are reading this book. Prepare for a significant change for the better in your life. One of the most significant changes in your life will be the tremendous contribution you will make in the lives of others in need. You were born to meet a need. Do you realize that you are in great demand?[3]

Chapter 1

Let God Restore Your Soul

We tune up our cars, repair and paint our homes, and take vitamins for our bodies. We do this to preserve, repair, or restore to a like new condition. It's time for us to give attention to the invisible part of us, our spiritual life. God knew long before hand that we would need restoring and made provisions to restore our souls. Allow God to comfort and restore you as you read this chapter.

He restores my soul; He leads me in the paths of righteousness For His name's sake (Ps. 23:3 NKJV).

God is a restorer who desires to continually restore us during life. In Psalm 23:3 the Word teaches us that God restores our soul. While on the run for his life, David was inspired by God to write this Psalm. He acknowledged God as the restorer of his soul.

Blessed be God, even the Father of our Lord Jesus Christ, the Father of mercies, and the God of all comfort; <u>Who comforteth us in all our tribulation</u>, that we may be able to comfort them which are in any trouble, by the comfort wherewith we ourselves are comforted of God (2 Cor. 1:3-4).

What does "restore my soul" mean?

The word restore in Hebrew is *Shub*, which means to refresh and relieve, to convert and deliver. The word restore has application to believers and unbelievers. Believers need to be refreshed and relieved. Unbelievers need to be converted and delivered. The word soul in Hebrew is *Nephesh*, which means life, desire, passion, or appetite. Therefore God converts and delivers (restores) the life, desires, passions, and appetites (soul) of the unbeliever. He refreshes and relieves the life, desires, and passions of the believer.

When is restoration needed?

We need restoration, at one time or another during our lives. We may experience greater than usual challenges, especially during present times of tension with the current security and economic situations. Many were burnout from the rigors of daily living before these recent incidents occurred.

We may be in need of restoration because our lives may have been stripped of the protective covering we once trusted. If so, we are in need of restoration. God allows stripping (or pruning) for our good. The first step in restoring furniture is to strip off the old in order to restore with the new.

> Every branch in me that beareth not fruit he taketh away: and every branch that beareth fruit, he purgeth it, that it may bring forth more fruit (John 15:2).

A healthy and positive attitude is critical, once we've been purged or stripped. We must allow God to restore our soul in order that we may bear more fruit and go farther than we would have gone if we had not been stripped. God offers an invitation to those who have been stripped as indicated in the following scripture:

> Come unto me, all ye that labour and are heavy laden, and I will give you rest [restore]. Take my yoke upon you, and learn of me; for I am meek and lowly in heart: and ye shall find rest [restoration] unto your souls. For my yoke is easy, and my burden is light (Matt. 11:28-30).

We may need restoration after being emotionally wounded by someone we trusted or respected. Such wounds if not soon healed [restored], may have a crippling affect on future relationships. The proper attitude to have towards such an experience is to realize that God may have allowed it to happen, not to hurt us, but to strengthen and mature us. In some cases, God may have attempted to prevent us from entering the relationship, knowing beforehand the outcome. But we may have persisted against His will. Nevertheless, He is merciful and desires to restore our soul from a wounded heart.

Our soul may need restoring after a failure. We may have failed in doing something which we expected to succeed. Perhaps we may be premature in judging it as a failure. Even though failure is experienced, we are not a failure. Again, a proper attitude is essential. We must allow God to restore us by learning from our mistakes rather than dwelling on them and immediately turn our attention and focus on future success with God. Every great man and woman of God failed numerous times in their lives, but they didn't quit. God counts us as faithful not as a failure.

> And I thank Christ Jesus our Lord, who hath enabled me, for that he counted me faithful, putting me into the ministry (1 Tim. 1:12).

Those in adverse environments whether at home, work, et cetera may be in need of God to regularly restore their soul. A person in an adverse environment may feel that they are in it alone and there is little or no hope. God desires to fight our battles for us. God is for us. God is victorious at everything He does. But God knows we can handle it, as long as we keep our trust in Him. Your environment may seem overwhelming to the eye or ear. God restores you, as you look not at the things, which are seen, but at the things that are not seen. God restores you as you realize that they who are with you are more than those who are against you.

How are we restored?

1. By one another (a joyous person refreshes you)

We can sharpen and refresh one another. God can use a friend or ally to bring refreshing to you. Therefore, it is beneficial to have as one of your friends a person who is always joyous or one who has the motivational gift of exhorter (encourager). We become like those with whom we associate with most. It may be wise to check your companions to determine if they are partners (helping you) or parasites (sucking life out of you).

> For we have great joy and consolation in thy love, because the bowels of the saints are refreshed by thee, brother. Yea, brother, let me have joy of thee in the Lord: refresh my bowels in the Lord (Philem. 1:7, 20).

> That I may come unto you with joy by the will of God, and may with you be refreshed (Rom. 15:32).

> Therefore we were comforted in your comfort: yea, and exceedingly the more joyed we for the joy of Titus, because his spirit was refreshed by you all (2 Cor. 7:13).

2. By the Word of God

For precept must be upon precept, precept upon precept; line upon line, line upon line; here a little, and there a little: For with stammering lips and another tongue will he speak to this people. To whom he said, This is the rest wherewith ye may cause the weary to rest; and this is the refreshing: yet they would not hear. But the word of the LORD was unto them precept upon precept,

precept upon precept; line upon line, line upon line; here a little, and there a little (Isa. 28:10-13)

The Word of God restores and revives us. Since the Word of God is *spirit and life*, it is a life giving or reviving source. We should spend quality time doing the following three things:

<u>Hearing the Word of God</u>. Faith comes by hearing and hearing by the Word of God. The Word of God is truth. When we know the truth of the Word of God, it makes us free. God gives us pastors to feed us with knowledge and understanding. We need to hear the Word of God taught and preached to have faith to believe and please God.

<u>Meditating on the Word of God</u>. We are to meditate (roll over in the mind) God's Word. For as a man thinks in his heart so is he (Proverbs 23:7). We become what we think about or meditate on most. We must exercise stewardship over our thought life by bringing every thought into the obedience of Christ. Our minds must be renewed by the Word of God so that we can prove the good, acceptable, and perfect will of God. Meditating on the Word of God is required for us to observe all that is written in the Word and have good success.

<u>Reading the Word of God</u>. We must read and study the Word in order to show ourselves approved unto God. Then we can rightly divide (understand) it. In order to be strong Christians we must know the Word. Reading the Word of God for ourselves gives

us more confidence in the Word and God. Plead my cause and redeem me; revive me according to Your Word (Ps. 119:154 NKJV).

3. By the presence of the God

Repent ye therefore, and be converted, that your sins may be blotted out, when the times of refreshing shall come from the presence of the Lord (Acts 3:19).

God Himself is the ultimate refresher. God never sleeps or slumbers (see Psalm 121:4). Therefore, weariness is not in God's character or nature. God is a creator. God is a healer. God is a builder. God is a restorer. The more time we spend in God's presence, the more we become like Him.

4. By praising God

To appoint unto them that mourn in Zion, to give unto them beauty for ashes, the oil of joy for mourning, the garment of praise for the spirit of heaviness; that they might be called trees of righteousness, the planting of the LORD, that he might be glorified (Isa. 61:3).

Praising God is magnifying God. It is boasting, bragging, or singing about whom He is and His character. The more we focus on God, the more we realize His ability. Praises cause us to see our problems and circumstance more like God sees them. Therefore, we realize that God is much bigger than our circumstances and realize that Jesus has already won our victory over them. We do not praise God for the negative circumstances.

> **We praise God in spite of the negative circumstance.**

These methods are not all inclusive. However, you will experience a greater degree of God's restoration in your life by spending time with someone who is full of faith, reading and studying the Bible, and vocally praising God for who He is. Don't delay! Get started now and make it a daily priority.

Chapter 2

Be Sure of Your Foundation

If you sense that your life has gotten off track, you're not enjoying life, or you're not experiencing the grace of God as you once did, go back to the foundation. Go to God. Allow Him to take you back to the beginning or where things began to get off track. He is the author of your faith.[4] Go back to the cornerstone on which the building of your life should rest.[5] Please notice that I did not say go back to programs, procedures, or people. Go back to the person, Jesus Christ. If you follow programs, procedures, or people without following Jesus you'll regret it sooner or later. Follow the person (Jesus). He'll connect you with the right program, procedure, and people.

Resume nurturing your relationship with Him.[6] Persist in pursuing Him. Spend time talking (praying) to your heavenly Father. Worship Him! Thank Him every moment you can. He treasures the thirty seconds you give Him. He treasures the thirty minutes you spend with Him in the morning, during your lunch break, or at night. Spend quality time with Him.

It's so easy to please Him, because what He treasures is you. He gave His utmost for you. Return to your first love.[7] He desires a two-way love relationship, Him loving you and you loving Him. His love for you motivated Him to give His life for you. He wants you to love Him back. Go back! Make time for Him! He is not difficult to get along with, and He's easy to talk to. He's down to earth, and will honor the sincerity of your heart.

> **Give Him back what rightfully belongs to Him, which is you.**

Chapter 3

Communicate with God

Prayer is man's method of communication with God. The more frequent we communicate with God the better prepared we are for life and life's circumstances. You may not be fully prepared in the natural (clothes, homes, finances, knowledge, or equipment). If we maintain consistent open communication with God, we'll be able to deal with any circumstance. Society in general typifies how important it is to communicate. Our environment is flooded with communication mediums (cell phones, radios, televisions, newspapers, magazines, dictionaries, encyclopedias, books, e-mail, Internet, billboards, posters, t-shirts, hats, et cetera). The deterioration of relationships begins with a breakdown in communication. In contrast, improving communication can strengthen a relationship. Communication significantly enhances effectiveness. It is essential to unity. The more frequent and effective the communication process, the more powerful are the parties who communicate.

Communication may be written, verbal, or nonverbal. In every environment or culture, one form will be used more than others, and progressive use of all available forms makes an effective culture. God is excellent in all His forms of communication. We identify with Him most by what He has written. The most readily form of communication God has made available to us is His written Word (the Bible). The Bible doesn't just contain God's Word. It is God's Word. It is God's written communication to humanity. When God created man He communicated with him. He instructed Adam to name all the animals in order to identify them. Communication is essential to identity. Whomever you communicate with frequently, you're able to identify with them and they can identify with you.

> **It's difficult to identify with someone you don't communicate with.**

This is why we say, "once I got to know him or her they were not like I thought at all." We discover this during the communication process. Without proper communication we may make invalid assumptions or incorrect identity.

We identify with athletes by how they perform athletically. We identify with singers based on what or how they sing. We identify with governors based upon how they govern. We identify with actors based on the roles they play. We identify with writers based upon what or how they write. All of us are better in one form of communication or expression than another.

God used prophets, kings, and apostles to write His Word. They wrote under the inspiration of the Holy Spirit what the Father, the Son, and the Holy Spirit said and did. Paul alone wrote two-thirds of the New Testament. Paul is most identified based upon what he spoke and did. Paul's writings are most inspiring. He captured his experiences, his thoughts, and his ambitions in written form. He is not noted as a great author. He never intended to be a great author. He communicated through writing as God moved him. He believed that his writing was as much of his duty to God as was his oral teaching. Therefore, his obedience in writing is to our benefit. Each of his writings had an immediate addressee (Galatians, Ephesians, Corinthians, Timothy, Titus, et cetera), yet they reached the entire world. They prove to be timeless direction, inspiration, and correction to humanity.

Communication produces direction. After communicating with a superior we receive direction. After communicating with God through prayer, we're focused on being, and doing what He purposed. We stay connected to our power source (God) through prayer. Every time Jesus came out of prayer, He did powerful things (healed the sick, cast out demons, raised the dead, and walked on water). Prayer propelled Paul to write two-thirds of the New Testament. Paul said, "I thank God that I pray in the spirit more than you all." John was in the spirit (in communication with God) on the Lord's Day and God gave him revelations, which he wrote in the book of Revelation. Smith Wigglesworth, the noted apostle of faith from England, performed healing miracles after coming out of prayer. Daniel prayed three times a day and he was a man of an excellent spirit. Elijah prayed and it did not rain for three years. He prayed again and the drought ended. We're encouraged to communicate with God and expect an answer with great and mighty results (Jeremiah 33:3).

What do you do after communicating with God in prayer? Identify your pattern of activity after communicating with God and discover what God is prompting and propelling you to do.

CHAPTER 4

MAKE PRAYER A PRIORITY

The Bible teaches that Jesus continued all night in prayer" (Luke 6:12). The next day He chose His disciples. Our prayers make us powerful. Praying makes us fruitful. Prayer gives us insight. We need to have a diligent prayer life. Prayer is an essential key and priority element in the believer's life (Matthew 7:7-8, 11).

Prayer should be the first thing we do on all occasions. Plan all events and occasions out of prayer. Most fruitlessness is due to a lack of prayer. Prayer produces greater intimacy with God. It is the best remedy for burn out. Increase your prayer time and get recharged and refreshed (Luke 18:1, Philippians 4:6).

Get serious—pray.

If you're not praying about it, you may not be serious about it. Prayer indicates that it's absolutely necessary to involve God. Prayer indicates that I need more than mere human strength and intellect. Prayer indicates that I am aiming for tremendous results and success. Prayer indicates that it's too costly to rely on man alone. Prayer indicates that there is only so much that I can do and that's not good enough. Prayer indicates that I trust and rely on the counsel, ability, and power of God (Psalm 118:4-9).

CHAPTER 5

BE WILLING AND READY TO CHANGE

True change in us can be achieved by following someone who is constant. Thank God that He doesn't change. Because of His consistency, we always know how to find Him and what He expects. Imagine if we were traveling on a journey and the destination and directions constantly changed. We'd be lost and confused, spending a lot of energy but not going anywhere. When the destination and directions remain unchanged, no matter how often or far we get off course we can always rely on the directions and have hope in the destination.

We were created for change. That's why babies don't stay babies. We progress through constant stages of development and maturity. We strive for this at an early age. Babies are eager to walk. Children are eager to ride a bike or swim. Teenagers are eager to drive or finish school. God placed this natural desire for change within us. Therefore, it is spiritually healthy for us to be in a changing environment.

As we reach natural maturity, we tend to become creatures of habit, despising change. We become complacent and settle far short of our destination. As we mature, less change happens naturally as when we are growing up. It then becomes our responsibility to change. Now we must want to change and be willing to work on change. Before we became adults, this happened naturally and we loved it. In fact, we despised our parents if they disagreed with us changing. Jesus used the example of a little child that He placed before the disciples.

> And said, Verily I say unto you, except ye be converted, and become as little children, ye shall not enter into the kingdom of heaven. Whosoever therefore shall humble himself as this little child, the same is greatest in the kingdom of heaven. And whoso shall receive one such little child in my name receiveth me (Matt. 18:3-5).

A child is humble and wants to grow up more than anything else. I believe Jesus is saying that we must remain as a child in this sense; always humble ourselves and want to grow up (change).

Change is painful to human nature. But the real you (the spirit) loves change. The Bible teaches us in John 3:8: "The wind bloweth where it listeth, and thou hearest the sound thereof, but canst not tell whence it cometh, and whither it goeth: so is every one that is born of the Spirit." The Spirit moves (changes) us.

Change produces life. God created Adam's physical stature, which would have remained unchanged, until God breathed the breath of life into him. Our change toward God gives evidence of the life of God in us. When the disciples vowed to follow Jesus wherever He went, His response was Matthew 8:20, "And Jesus saith unto him, The foxes have holes, and the birds of the air have nests; but the Son of man hath no where to lay His head." Jesus was saying, I'm always on the move (so be ready for change).

When we experience complacency it grieves our heart. One of the saddest things is for us to see people who have been saying and doing the same thing for years, without change. People who do not want to change may despise you when you change. They may want you to remain as they are or whom they are familiar with. That's why they often remind you of whom you were and what you use to do. Too often we talk of where we've been instead of where we're going. Even when we fellowship with one another, we talk more about yesterday or yesteryear than tomorrow. The Bible teaches us not to say that the former days were better. No matter how good it's been, I believe God wants us to have a "the best is yet to come" attitude. The Pharisees and Sadducees didn't want to change, because they thought they had arrived. Jesus opposed them strongly. God opposes complacency. Tradition or lack of change will stop the work of God's Word in our life.

Inner change automatically produces outer change. In fact, recognition of inner change can cause us to change our attitude about the external. For example, the exterior appearance of a house may be in poor condition, causing our overall opinion of it to be negative. If we enter it and discover that it's beautiful on the inside our opinion of the entire house changes. Then we develop a more positive attitude about the house based on its interior condition oppose to its exterior appearance. It's very misleading if a house is beautiful on the exterior only. The lawn is beautifully landscaped, but it's interior is deteriorated. True quality is measure by the condition of the interior. If the interior components are maintained then it will function properly.

Jesus said in Matthew 12:43-45, "When the unclean spirit is gone out of a man, he walketh through dry places, seeking rest, and findeth none. Then he saith, I will return into my house from whence I came out; and when he is come, he findeth it empty, swept, and garnished. Then goeth he, and taketh with himself seven other spirits more wicked than himself, and they enter in and dwell there: and the last state of that man is worse than the first. Even so shall it be also unto this wicked generation." Notice that the unclean spirit takes up residency within a man not outside. It doesn't matter how the man is dressed, his facial expression, or even what he says. If there is no change of the inner man, then even a worse condition occurs.

This is the soul of man: He strives for and pays great emphasis and exertion on the outer appearance of things. Even when he achieves the desired outer appearance, he's still not satisfied. The reason why he's still not satisfied is because he is not fulfilled within. He saw the fruit on the outside and focused his efforts on the fruit because that's what everyone else will see. The world commends and rewards exterior appearance while God rewards and commends man's internal appearance (the heart). A marriage ceremony is an example of an outward expression of an inner change in relationship between a man and a woman.

Change your mind by renewing it according to God's Word and your behavior will change automatically. As Job said, "the root of the matter is in me." The responsibility for the matter lies with me. The location of the matter is in me. Change the root and the fruit will follow.

CHAPTER 6

THE HOLY SPIRIT WILL HELP YOU CHANGE

The Holy Spirit is the person who helps us change into who we should be, which is more like Christ. He is the power of God working in us. He is the voice of God counseling and teaching us. He is the unction of God leading us.

We should lean on the Holy Spirit, trust Him, depend upon Him, rely upon Him, use Him, and consult Him. You and I cannot lift a finger for Christ without the Holy Spirit. He is invaluable, most necessary, and critical for believers to be successful in Christ. "Please, allow the Holy Spirit to do His job in your life." He may not lead you in the way you want to go. However, He will lead and guide you in the way you should go. He is involved in every victory and every promise you receive.

He is the Spirit of grace. He is the grace of God. He imparts the grace of God in our lives daily and seasonally. He is the agent of change. He is the Spirit of change in the believer. Love Him and love on Him. Your lives will become much more fruitful as you appreciate Him more.

He'll help you help you.

Jesus knew we'd need help. He didn't just send help (the verb form), He sent a Helper (the noun form) to abide with us. Help is limited by occasion and circumstance. Whenever we need help (which is daily) we should solicit the Helper (the Holy Spirit).

The Holy Spirit is the one who wrote (through John) to the seven churches (Revelation chapter two). It begins with, "He who has an ear let him hear what the SPIRIT says." For example, He wrote to Thyatria, the corrupt church and helped them by identifying corrective actions the church should take. In like manner, the Holy Spirit helps churches and individuals today.

He is available, willing, and waiting to help you change. He is an expert at helping people change. He knows what areas you need to change and how to effectively change you. I believe He's working change in you right now.

CHAPTER 7

SET YOUR MIND TO IT

You can do anything, if you set your mind to it. For as a man thinks in his heart so is he (Proverbs 23:7). If your life is in a pit, get your mind out first. The rest will follow. If you get your mind pointed in the right direction, it's only a matter of time before everything else follows. Get your mind off trouble. Get your mind off worry. Get your mind off sickness. Get your mind off your enemies. Get your mind off your bills. Get your mind off your shortcomings. Get your mind off educational limitations. Get your mind off what your husband, your wife, or your children are not. Get your mind pointed in the right direction (Philippians 4:6-8). The results will certainly follow.

You have a solution available for problems, guaranteed by God Himself. It will bring peace to your mind more effective than any medication, without side effects. Your solution is in God's opinion about you and your situations. It is God's promise concerning you. It is God's way to solving every situation in life. It is God's Word, the Bible, the written Word of God. Start saying what it says rather than what you see, feel, or hear from people that contradict the Word. Keep saying what the Word says daily, over and over again! Overwhelm your mind with God's Word, "And do not be conformed to this world, but be transformed by the renewing of your mind, that you may prove what is that good and acceptable and perfect will of God" (Rom. 12:2 NKJV).

Overwhelm your mind with God's Word.

Chances are you already don't like most of what you've been thinking. You haven't been able to take control of your thoughts because you're in a fight and you've been fighting with the wrong weapons. You're in a faith fight! You have an adversary sending thoughts into your mind, which are contrary to what God desires and plans for you. You haven't been able to overcome your thoughts because you haven't put up a fight against those thoughts with God's thoughts, which is His Word. Only God's Word can defeat those thoughts. Only God's Word can bring peace into your mind. Constant peace!

The battle in your mind is more important than the battle in your body, or the battle in your home. When you win the battle in your mind, you've won the battle. You must win the mental battle first. After winning the mind battle, you'll discover that you don't have a physical battle that can defeat you, you've already won.

> But thanks be to God, who gives us the victory through our Lord Jesus Christ (1 Cor. 15:57 NKJV).

Stop blaming yourself for your problems. Don't let anyone else blame you. Stop blaming others for your problems. Jesus took the blame. The blame was nailed to the cross. Don't bear the blame. He died for you and every problem you have or will have. You've been set free by the blood of Jesus. Now meditate on that. Think about it, day in and day out. Start talking about what Jesus has done more than what you see or feel. Allow Jesus the final say concerning you. Put your mind to it!

Jesus took the blame but you take the responsibility for believing and receiving what He has done for you. Put up a fight using the weapons of your warfare, which is God's Word. Commit yourself to reading and speaking His Word throughout each day. Put your mind to it. It is the best thing you can do for your family, for yourself, and the body of Christ.

We're all counting on you to fight the good fight.

> Fight the good fight of faith, lay hold on eternal life, to which you were also called and have confessed the good confession in the presence of many witnesses (1 Tim. 6:12 NKJV).

Use the weapon God gave you, the Word. God designated a weapon that cannot be defeated and has not been defeated. Others can, will, and should pray for you.

No one can fight for you, like you can fight for you.

So fight the good fight! You've already won! You're already victorious. God says so.

> Now thanks be to God who always leads us in triumph in Christ, and through us diffuses the fragrance of His knowledge in every place (2 Cor. 2:14 NKJV).

> Yet in all these things we are more than conquerors through Him who loved us (Rom. 8:37 NKJV).

If you don't keep your mind on the Word you'll think you're defeated, less than, weak, poor, or sick. The Word says otherwise. So put the thoughts of God in your mind and keep them there. God has declared that you're more than a conquer, an overcomer, and always triumph in Christ Jesus. It sounds like you've won. Keep your victory by keeping your mind on the Word. The devil is trying to steal your victory by making you think you're not victorious. God says you are. Therefore, you are! Yes You Are!

So put your mind to it. Tell yourself, "I'm going to think what God thinks, and I'm going to say what God says." Daily read and say what God has said about you.

For I know the thoughts that I think toward you, saith the LORD, thoughts of peace, and not of evil, to give you an expected end (Jeremiah 29:11).

I am come that they might have life, and that they might have it more abundantly (John 10:10).

Declare that Jesus has given you this authority. Use His name (Jesus) and take charge over the circumstances in your life.

And whatsoever ye shall ask in my name, that will I do, that the Father may be glorified in the Son (John 14:13).

"Behold, I give unto you power to tread on serpents and scorpions, and over all the power of the enemy: and nothing shall by any means hurt you" (Luke 10:19).

You can do anything, if you put your mind to it!

Chapter 8

Don't Be Paralyzed by Past Mistakes

I believe God is saying "it's ok" if you believed you heard Him and acted in faith, even though you missed Him. At least you are moving and willing to move and change with God. God can do more with you than someone who is paralyzed by fear of missing God.

Don't fret if you've thought you heard God and acted upon it and later learned that it wasn't God. Keep seeking God. Pray about it. God's directions will be in agreement with the scriptures. Don't be afraid to make a mistake. Learn from your mistakes. If you've gotten off track, get back on and keep moving forward with God. Learn to forget those things, which are behind you, acknowledge that you missed it, and reach forward to those things, which are ahead.

You've dwelt on your mistakes too long. You may even think others are focused on your mistakes. They have their own mistakes and challenges. Your mistakes are in the past. Keep them there. God counted you faithful, you need to say you're faithful. God is faithful to forgive you of your sin (mistakes) and cleanse you from all unrighteousness. A just man may fall seven times, but he rises up again (Proverbs 24:16).

God isn't like many coaches — if you missed a shot, they take you out of the game. If you've been on the bench or sideline of life watching everyone else play, there is a new game and God wants you to start. Allow God to coach you. He's been coaching you even while you were out of the game. Let Him call the plays and you run the plays He calls. He wants you to study His play-book, the Bible. So, when He calls a play you'll be familiar with it.

As you pursue Him and the leading (not pushing) of the Holy Spirit, your entire life and experiences will be filled with the light, life, and love of God. God will pour life into you and your love ones. Forget those things you tried, people you trusted, or places you dwelt which were mistakes. Live now and in the future. God is full of hope and success. Get your rightful share of it.

> **Because you missed it in the past does not mean you will miss it in the future.**

Don't become stagnate! Don't sit idle! God is anointing you with fresh oil. Be diligent to pray. Be full of faith in what Jesus has already done for you and pursue

Him with purpose and passion. Expect yourself to succeed instead of fail. Tell yourself that you know God's voice and the voice of a stranger you will not follow. Spend quality time reading and studying the Word of God. Begin now!

Chapter 9

Learn from Life's Mistakes

God will allow things or people we trust in to fail us. He will allow us to come to naught, experience failure, so that we may realize that it or they have failed us and our trust is in something other than Him. He's God enough and loves enough to let us experience failure in order to show us where our faith lies.

Do you remember a community that blossomed and was prosperous years ago, but, today it's impoverished? Have you admired people who seemed to have it going on, but now they are worse off than you are? The same holds true for people and things you see today. Their prominence will fade away unless they are anchored, built, and abide in Jesus. Except the Lord builds the house, they who build it labor in vain (Psalm 127:1).

You may not have built a golden calf to worship. But, perhaps you have and worship something less tangible. Whatever it is, it will inevitably let you down, if you have hope in it. From time to time in life, we will put our trust in someone or something that fails us.

When you fail, you become analytical about it. You dissect every component of it. You carefully review who, what, when, how, and why. You evaluate motives. Progress begins when you stop blaming someone else for the mistake and accept responsibility. You begin to learn more about yourself and corrections you need to make. The more you correct yourself, the greater you benefit from your mistake. Analyze yourself based upon the Word of God. It will counsel you to forgive others who may have contributed to your mistake. It will strengthen you to love others unconditionally.

We're not to stop hoping because of our mistakes and failures. We're to learn from it and move on. It was not the thing or the person who failed us. It was our hope or faith, in them or it, that failed us. The thing or person did all they were capable, with limited imperfect qualities. We hoped in something which was not capable of being produced by what or whom we trusted in. God is unlimited. His abilities are endless. As we refocus our attention and trust on Him, He fulfills and exceeds every biblical expectation we can have of Him. He is irreplaceable. God is dependable and reliable. Trust in Him. It's easy to trust in Him. Thank Him for the people and things He gives us. No matter how big your failure, God can work it for your good.

CHAPTER 10

BREAK DOWN YOUR RELATIONSHIP WALLS

During our lives we've built invisible but strong walls between others. These walls were constructed with the materials of hurt, offense, rejection, discrimination, failure, et cetera. The list goes on and on. For the most part these walls were built on one side, our side. In most cases the other person or group doesn't know a wall exists. They may simply realize that things are not the way they once were.

We have maintained these walls well by going the other way and avoiding communication or contact at all expense. We maintain these walls of separation through continual feeding on the wrong or impression of wrong done. We visit these walls daily, weekly, or in some cases, hourly. The wall has become a wall of self-pity and excuses. In more sever cases the wall has become a wall of justification of self-abuse, abuse or mistreatment of others. We hold the sole title and deed of ownership of the wall we've built.

The wall is constructed by us intending to keep a certain person or group of people out and at a distance. However, the wall by nature not only keeps out what is undesired it also keeps out others whom we're trying to draw in. The wall may be keeping out a husband, wife, or child. It may be keeping out a friend or potential employer (promotion). The wall also keeps out dreams, visions, and ideas leading to a successful future. The wall represents and is held together with the glue of the past.

Our walls also keep us in. Thereby, preventing us from moving forward. Our range is kept at bay tied to the wall using the rope of the past. We're limiting ourselves in friendships and relationships. Since misery loves company, we unintentionally or intentionally enclose those close to us in the same wall. Thereby, limiting their potential.

Breaking down these walls is a key to success. It releases us and those whom we've tried to keep out. The longer we allow the wall to exist, the longer we delay our successful future. Have you witnessed bereaving relatives or friends regretting not having made things right (broken down the wall) with their loved ones while they had a chance? The fallacy is that we think the wall is hurting the other person, while it's not. It's hurting us.

There is one thing that keeps us from approaching the wall with the sledgehammer of forgiveness to destroy it. The one thing is pride. Pride says I will not. Pride says

I cannot. Pride says it's not my fault. Pride says I have a right not to forgive them and restore the relationship. Pride says I've done fine without them so far. Pride says I'll go to my grave before I make it right with them. Pride costs. It costs us anxiety. It costs us aging. It costs us health. It costs us one of the most valuable things on earth, another person (1 Peter 5:6).

People are valuable to God. He sent His son Jesus to die for you and for the person or persons you have decided to build a wall between. God is with you where you are now. God is also with that person on the other side of your wall.

Man is well accustomed to building walls. Man through his disobedience built a wall between he and God. God said I love you too much to have a wall between us. That's what Jesus' life, death, and resurrection represents: I forgive you (break down the wall) no matter what you've done. He reconciled us to the Father. He commands us to break down walls between one another.

There is one thing that empowers us to do the right thing. The one thing is LOVE. Love says I forgive and release you. Love says I need you in my life. Love says I forgive you because I need forgiveness also. Love says you're worth it, no matter who you are or what you've done.

Allow the love in you to break down the walls you have built between others. Love them and care for their well-being just as you would desire for others to love you and be concerned about your well-being. Here are a few ways to help you get started.

Privately pray for them. Pray for them as earnestly as you would for yourself. Ask God to bless them, heal them, promote them, and be merciful towards them.

Purposely talk to them. Be kindly persistent. Your words of kindness work on their heart even if they appear to reject you.

Publicly praise them. Say positive things about them in the presence of others. Build them up in the eyes of others.

> **Be persistent. Be patient. Be loving.**
> **Be forgiving. Be kind. Be helpful.**
> **James 3:13-18**

CHAPTER 11

DON'T PUT YOUR TRUST
IN THINGS AROUND YOU

Joshua Chapter 6

The people of Jericho's trust, prominence, and security was in the magnificent wall around them. It was not in their ability to fight. I don't believe they planned to fight or knew how to fight. Perhaps they didn't even train to fight.

Their boast was no one can get in and no one can get out (Joshua 6:1). The wall was probably too high and upright for anyone to climb over without risking their life.

I can hear God saying to the people of Jericho, "first I'm going to deal with (destroy) what you've built around you, and then I'll deal with you." God doesn't want men to trust in a man-made structure. Examples are the tower of Babel, the golden calf, and the wall of Jericho.

God may allow your enemy to destroy what shouldn't be in your life. The people of Jericho were not that mighty, they had a mighty wall. The children of Israel were not that mighty, they had (and we have) a mighty God. We may look at people and think they're mighty because of what they have around them (e.g., a good job, a nice house, a nice car, fine clothing, live in an affluent community). They can easily be defeated if their trust is not in God.

Beyond the wall. If God can get us to see past the wall! All too often we see the wall and don't look or plan any further. The ten spies made such a mistake. The people are strong, the cities are walled and very great (Numbers 13:28).

Word walls. Sometimes people build a wall around them with their words (tough talk). They try to impress, intimidate, threaten, reject, or discourage you. God wants you to see past the wall.

The adversary wall. The devil builds a wall. He builds a wall of adverse circumstances and attacks against an abundant life. He goes about as a roaring lion. He has the appearance to be invincible. In the end, we shall look narrowly upon him and see just how incapable he is.

Silence. There's silence and then there's a sound. At Jericho, there was silence for six days, and then on the seventh day there was a sound. In Elijah's time, there was silence of rain for three and one-half years. There was a sound of abundance and it rained. After Malachi, there was silence. Then there was a sound with John the Baptist.

If God is silent in your life, there is a sound coming. When someone gets ready to begin a program, make an announcement, pray, or sing the national anthem, there is silence and then there's a sound. When a baby is conceived, there is nine months of silence, then there's a sound. God shuts us up before He lets us talk. Jesus was silent for thirty years on earth, and then He began to make a sound. Future ministers, leaders, musicians, and professionals are silent. In due time they'll make a sound.

Destroyed with a sound. God uses a sound to bring down walls. He uses sounds (words), which He instructed. At Jericho, He used the sound of the seven trumps and the shout of the children of Israel. At Babel, He used His own voice by saying "I will confuse their language." He used John the Baptist's cry to breakdown the wall of unrepentance so Jesus could fulfill His redemptive purpose. He used Peter's voice to break down the wall between Jews and Gentiles.

Joshua was God's leader. His success depended upon the Word of God in him. Joshua chapter one verse eight states, "This book of the law shall not depart out of your mouth; but, you shall meditate in it day and night, that you may observe to do all that is written in it, then you will make your way prosperous and have good success." God instructed Joshua to have the Word in him, which ensured He would lead them to destroy Jericho.

CHAPTER 12

ESTABLISH SCREENING
CRITERIA FOR YOUR LIFE

You should establish quality control measures for your life. There should be a screening process to control what enters and exits your life. This ensures that you consistently produce quality results through life.

Routinely, you apply screening or evaluating criteria in making purchases, decisions, and investments of time, resources, or money. You can do similarly with life by asking, how will this contribute, add value, or give me resources to fulfill the purpose for my life?

- Will it bless me or burden me?
- Will it help me or hinder me?
- Is it God inspired or only a good idea?

The Bible states that every good and perfect gift comes from above, down from the Father of lights and that the blessing of the Lord makes rich and adds no sorrow with it, nor does toiling increase it. [8]

Some things are meant to be in our lives for a moment (brief season), while others are meant to be lasting.[9] Holding on to something that is meant for a brief season may be costly to us once its season (fruitfulness) is over. Conversely, it may be costly if we release something prematurely that is meant to be in our life for a long time. Recognize the difference! This applies to possessions, relationships, inheritances, et cetera.

Evaluate the efficiency of your life. Are you spending energy on things, which have no return? If you're seeking, seek to find. If you're knocking, knock for it to be opened. If you're asking, ask for it to be given. Make sure you're toiling in the right soil in the right season for the right reason. The method that works for others may not be best for you. Evaluate!

Chapter 13

Calibrate Your Perspective

After ensuring that the things we are involved in add value to our lives, our perspective needs calibrating to ensure our attitude is consistent with God's. To calibrate means to adjust or make proper corrections for a particular function. Our perspective needs calibrating because our experiences and knowledge may have created an inaccurate view of others.

We should pray, asking God to give us the proper perspective of . . .

Ourselves	Our health
Our pastor	Our spouse
Our job	Our church
Our children	Our city
Our prosperity	The lost
The backslidden	The saved

Ask (invite) and allow God to give you the proper perspective.[10] It allows God to reveal the truth to us. Invite Him to correct faulty attitudes and beliefs about yourself and others. As He reveals the proper perspective it is incumbent upon us to make the needed changes to correct it. Otherwise, you deceive yourself. We become like a man who observes himself in a mirror, goes away and immediately forgets his true reflection in the mirror.[11]

This calibration establishes a plumb line for our lives.[12] If the plumb line is inaccurate, the whole building (our lives) will not be properly constructed. Our plumb line is our perspective (how we see things). If we don't see things accurately, we can't respond accurately. We have a perspective about everything in our lives. We are living our lives based upon our perspective. We may be wasting time and resources because of an inaccurate perspective. For starters, we need to seek a proper perspective of ourselves. We're not as hopeless as we may think. We're not as incapable as we may think. Our situation is not too far-gone as we may think. On the other hand, we may not be as on target as we think. We need to ask God for His perspective of our situation and us. Find it in the Word of God where it's written concerning us. It is written in the Word of God that we can do all things through Christ Jesus. It is also written that "if God be for us, who can be against us."[13] Since you have so much ahead of you to do, it's vital to begin with the proper perspective.

CHAPTER 14

KNOW YOU'RE CARED ABOUT

As mentioned before, the methods that work for others may not work for you. God uses different methods to carry out His plans. We should not depend on methods. If it's not working for you, it doesn't mean that God doesn't care about you. Perhaps it means that He cares about you so much that He will not allow what is not meant for you to work for you. [14]

God cannot be replicated or duplicated. He is an original and He created us as originals. He created everyone different. Realize and accept yourself as an original. Allow God's love and compassion to comfort you and others around you. Appreciate the differences and uniqueness in others, opposed to distancing yourself from them and looking for others like you. The world is full of people looking for someone who cares and loves them unconditionally. As you apprehend the love Christ has for you personally, you'll love others as He loves them.

As a child, you may not have experienced having someone who cared for you affectionately. So you grew up vulnerable to those who pretended to care for you. Perhaps they used you to fulfill their selfish motives. Not knowing or having experienced genuine care, you fall for pretenders. Your life may consist of going from relationship to relationship with those who are only pretending to care, relationships with friends, employers, or Christians.

Consequently, it may be difficult for you to believe that someone could care for you affectionately and unconditionally with no strings attached. But, that's the only kind of care God gives. The bottom line is, that people of all walks of life genuinely want, need, and yearn for someone who cares for them affectionately and watchfully, as Jesus does. He is a friend who sticks closer than a brother. However, He uses people like you to express this care for one another. In order for you to genuinely and truly express it His way, you must receive and daily live in the care He has for you personally. Then you can change the world, one person at a time by the care you have for others. Jesus is a passionate person and we should be passionate people. Care is powerful. It protects. It heals. It rescues. It delivers. It forgives. Please allow the Lord to express His care for you.

Chapter 15

Don't Neglect Yourself

Make taking good care of yourself a priority. The better care you take of yourself the more energy, enthusiasm, and endurance you'll have to share with your family and others. Unfortunately, we tend to abuse ourselves with inadequate rest or an unbalanced diet. One thing we neglect most is doing wholesome things that are fun, enjoyment and relaxation for us. For example, writing and fishing are two things I get such benefits from. I get great fulfillment and sense of accomplishment from writing, while fishing is fun and relaxing. As I schedule these events into my activities, I have more joy to share and spread to my loved ones and a clear understanding of how I can contribute to the success of others.

There are numerous things that cry for our attention. We cry for attention. This cry is a cry of self-pity, which may lead to self-indulgence of some sort.

Disciplining ourselves is our greatest challenge. We must refuse to be lazy, procrastinate, or have a lackadaisical attitude. Make yourself do better and be better. Metaphorically speaking, prepare a meal, rather than just go into the kitchen and throw something together. Stop waiting for someone else to make things happen for you. Get busy and become aggressive at making it happen. Become a source for others to come to for guidance, service, or support.

Come out of the corner you've been backed into for so long. You can come out! Be determined! Work at it bit by bit, little by little, consistently. Don't downplay your ability. The little you can do is big to someone in need.

Have fun! Enjoy every step you can. You are responsible for your fun as much as you're responsible for your work. The better you take care of yourself, the more effective you'll be at helping others. So, take care.

CHAPTER 16

DISTINGUISH YOUR ADVERSARIES FROM YOUR ALLIES

There are people we have contact with who present themselves as our allies — ready, willing, and able to help us. They may present us with a sales pitch, intended for us to buy in to their proposal. They may even befriend us. Who doesn't welcome a friendly person? In some cases they appear to be the answer to prayers. Are they luring us with hidden motives? The Bible gives numerous scriptures on the nature of people up to no good. The following examples in the books of Ezra chapter four and Nehemiah chapter six are useful references in distinguishing adversaries from allies.

When they hear of your progress (success) . . .
They say, let us build with you.

They're not interested in working for you. They want equal credit and authority with you.

They say, we seek your God as you do.

> They realize you seek God. So they use religious phraseology to woo you. He's yet to become their God.

They try to discourage you and trouble you in your building by: employing counselors against you to frustrate your purpose.[15]

> They don't send attackers to physically tear down your work. They see you as purpose driven so they get people to start questioning and second-guessing your purpose.

They say, come let us meet together but they plan to do you harm.

> They want to dialogue instead of work. They want to get an opportunity for you to entertain their proposals.

They send messengers again and again.[16]

> They send others with messages, instead of coming themselves.

The response . . .

You may do nothing with us to build a house for our God, but we alone will build to the Lord God of Israel.[17]

The response is direct and to the point.

I'm doing a great work and cannot come down. Why should the work cease while I leave it and go down to you?[18]

I will not be distracted or delayed from my purpose. If I come dialogue with you the work will cease. The work I'm doing takes priority over dialogue.

You will know them by their fruit.

CHAPTER 17

ATTRACT USING THE WORD OF GOD

Adorn your life, ambition, and pursuits with the Word of God. Let it be the hidden motive for why you live. Apply the Word of God as a business strategy, market plan, or road map.[19] Use it as your compass to success.

The Word of God attracts. It attracts health.[20] It attracts healing. It attracts prosperity.[21] It attracts favor. People will be drawn to you because of the desirable fruit produced by the Word. Some will come seeking the fruit, while others will come seeking the source of the fruit.

The Word of God is attractive.

The Word of God is a magnet for the promises of God. Conversely, it repels everything posing a threat to a fruitful life. The Word attracts the health, wealth, peace, joy, and fulfillment we desire. A person who possesses these things in their life is attractive. The fruit of the Word attract others (Proverbs 4:20-23).

The more we expose the Word of God to our ears, eyes, and thoughts it attracts the promises of God to us. God wants us to be attractive. We should be an attractive solution to those in need. What we say should be more attractive than what the profane and perverse say. Our lives should be more attractive than what the corrupt possess. When someone asks, how did we obtain it, we're able to say it is the Word of God. It makes the Word become attractive to them.

Chapter 18

Recognize God's Plans and Instructions

God's plan is always consistent with His nature and character. His Word contains His pattern of operation, which is the same yesterday, today, and forever. His method may change but His principles do not.

God makes His plans and instructions clear and plain to whom He's communicating. He does not want us confused, because He is not an originator of confusion. God leads us in a plain path. He is very specific and detailed as need be. Let's study some examples of how He provides instruction.

Jonah: "go to Nineveh and cry out against that city." God told Jonah which city to go to and what to do when he arrived. God needed him to go to Nineveh to cry out (or speak, teach/preach His Word; Jonah 1:2).

Elijah: "get away from here and turn eastward and hide by the brook Cherith, which flows into the Jordan. And it will be that you shall drink from the brook, and I have commanded the ravens to feed you there." God told Elijah where to go, how to get there, and how He (God) would feed him (1 Kings 17:2-4).

Elijah: "Arise, go to Zarephath, which belongs to Zidon, and dwell there. See, I have commanded a widow there to provide for you" (1 Kings 17:9). Once again God told Elijah where to go and how He (God) would sustain him.

In both cases, if Elijah had gone anywhere else other than where God instructed, God would not have been obligated to provide for him. However, once Elijah obeyed God's instruction, God faithfully provided accordingly. In contrast, Jonah did not follow God's instructions and he (Jonah) had to pay his fare (make his own provision; Jonah 1:3). Jonah later obeyed God and went to Nineveh.

Joshua: "You shall march around the city, all you men of war; you shall go around the city once. This you shall do six days. And seven priests shall bear seven trumpets of rams' horns before the ark. But the seventh day you shall march around the city seven times, and the priests shall blow the trumpets. It shall come to pass, when they make a long blast with the ram's horn, and when you hear the sound of the trumpet, that all the people shall shout with a great shout" Joshua 6:2-5. God instructed Joshua how to defeat the enemy at Jericho. He gave Joshua a plan or strategy, which required the obedience of Joshua and all participants. It was a sequential, time-phased strategy. The success of the plan relied on the ability of God once men carried out the plan.

Phillip: "Arise and go toward the south along the road which goes down from Jerusalem to Gaza, this is desert" (Acts 8:26).

God told Phillip the direction to travel. He even gave him the road to take and terrain (desert) associated with his trip.

Phillip: "Go near and overtake this chariot" (Acts 8:29). God further instructed Phillip to a specific chariot. Phillip got to this point by obeying previous instructions. First, God guided him to the general area He wanted him to be. Then He guided him to a specific chariot in that area. Once Phillip allowed God to lead him to the place and the person (or people), then he received an open door to preach the gospel. God sets before us an open door, which no man can close. He guides us to discover the open door.

We have reviewed several examples of how God gives us His plan and instructions. It's very apparent that God doesn't want us confused, nor does He attempt to confuse us. The Holy Spirit leads and guides us into all truth. God does not want us to be out of place or off the path. Our responsibility is to follow, in detail, His instructions for us. We have access to His instructions, which is His Word (the Bible). The more time we spend studying the Bible the clearer we'll hear and the more obedient we should become. He speaks to us through and consistent with His Word.

CHAPTER 19

TREASURE THE GRACE GOD HAS GIVEN YOU

The insight (revelation) and grace God gives you will be consistent with . . .

Your pursuit of Him.
The task in life He has for you.

You doing all things through Christ who strengthens you is equal to the above. Him enabling you is dependent upon your dedication to Him and His purpose for your life. He will not grace or strengthen you to be an anointed or gifted financial businessman if His purpose for you is to be a carpenter. Find and remain in the grace He has called you to at the level He has equipped you with. Then your life will have peace.

The more you sincerely seek Him, the more He leads you to the area of grace for your life. Be content with such things you have also means to be content with the grace and the path of grace God has given you. You will possess unusual wisdom in the area God has graced you with.

Appreciate others for their uniqueness and commitment to live a lifestyle which you do not have the grace or patience to do. Patience is a key indicator of your area of grace. You have great patience for the task. You have patience for the task, people, and the place associated or connected with your assignment in life. If your calling is to help others who are in despair, you have wisdom in how they're to do it and be patient with them doing it.

Chapter 20

Use What You Have

"Such as I have, give I unto thee."
Acts 3:6

There are hundreds and thousands sitting by the roadside of life waiting for someone to meet their daily need. You see and hear them everyday. Have you concluded that it's someone else's responsibility to respond? These people are your neighbors, your coworkers, your employers, your employees, and your relatives. They strategically place themselves so their needs are visible by those who would be most likely to assist them. They're seeking assistance through their conversation, through their attire, through their driving, through their solitude, and through their congeniality. They may think you're not struggling in the area of their need. Nevertheless, they have something to offer to you, their attention and the opportunity for you to give what you have.

Someone needs what you have. It was given to you for those in need. When you are approached you may not have what they ask for, but, you may have what they need. Someone may stop you to ask for directions, and you may not know of the location they're asking. Perhaps you can give them something helpful.

Everyone has something of great value. You may not have an abundance of material things but your know-how may be of great value. What is it that you do well with ease? What have you been doing for years, as a hobby or for pastime? What household or homemade skills do you have?

Such as you have! You have what it takes. You must see what you have to be of great value and importance. A gift is as a precious stone in the eyes of the possessor. You may know something that others need to know. You must be willing to offer what you have. Others will not know what you have until you offer service.

Take inventory of what you have.

- Acceptability is based upon what you have, not on what you don't have.

- The widow, who gave two mites, gave what she had.

What you have is much.

- To whom much is given, much is required.

- The seemingly little in your hands becomes much in others' hands. Use what you have.

The widow at Zarapeth thought she had nothing. But God used what she had. She had a little oil and meal with which she made what appeared to be their last meal. It turned out that what she had was all she needed.

Give what you have.

- What's in your possession? What's in your hand? God will use what you have.

- Jesus asked the disciples what they had to feed the multitude. He fed thousands with a little boy's lunch.

- List your God given abilities and gifts.

- List your possessions.

- Focus on what you have instead of what you don't have.

If you really need something, God would have given it to you or given you what you need to get it. The devil comes to steal, kill, and destroy. Since he wants to steal, it means you have something of value. Since he wants to kill and destroy it means that you are a threat to him.

When you're asked for what you don't have, you're asked based upon perceived need. You have a solution. People don't ask you based on the depth of their need. Doing so would expose their destituteness in this area. So when you're asked for assistance, it may be in generalities. Only during emergencies, in desperation we scream out the true nature of our needs. Their inquiry may be watered down by their loss of hope. Perhaps the man at the gate called Beautiful had lost the hope to walk and settled for daily sustenance opposed to divine health. Most people who do not expect to receive something don't even ask. However, those who expect to receive something usually ask. They're expecting to receive something from you. Your time and patience would be greatly welcomed, because many don't give those in need the time of day.

Those who preceded the "good Samaritan" to the scene didn't realize what they had. It wasn't by chance they passed by the robbed and injured man. Their error was seeing what they had as being exclusively for them and valuing it as a possession rather than a service. They even went so far as to pass by the other side of the road in effort to avoid being convicted by the injured looking upon them. There's nothing more convicting than someone looking upon you when you've denied or ignored them. Peter experienced this when he had denied Jesus three times. Jesus' words initially didn't correct Peter, but, His look did.

What you have to give is of great value. Begin to see it as valuable to others. God is allowing you to exercise stewardship over it. He's not allowing you to keep it to yourself. It's greatest benefit to you is discovered by using it to help others. Use what you currently possess and bless.

CHAPTER 21

FOLLOW THE PATH OF FAVOR

The Lord will lead you in a path of favor where He impresses upon the hearts of men to favor you. Others may labor or deceive to achieve. You receive because of the favor of the Lord. God favors you because He's in covenant with you. Favor is one way God shows you the path to follow. It is like a voice in your ear saying this is the way, walk in it.[22] He set before you open doors that no man can close.[23]

Meditate on the favor of God. We should think about and rely on the favor of God. It should be a part of our planning in life. We must expect it and anticipate receiving it.

God may have opened a door for you, but you may not be open to where the door is located.

Be cognizant of the favor of God. We need to be aware of the areas and paths in our lives, which were made possible by the favor of God. We need to do a historical analysis of the favor of God operating in our lives. Trace the locations, association, timing, and activities of favor. We will discover it is an outline leading to our God-given destiny.

You need to seek, knock, and ask in order to experience the favor of God. Most people don't seek because they don't expect to find, they expect doors to be closed, or they expect the answer will be no. You need to seek, go knock, and ask, expecting the favor of God. If at first you don't succeed, try again. The door or opportunity may be closed to everyone else, because it's reserved for you. God wants to show you His favor.

The favor of God increases you, leads to a closer relationship with God, gives you what you may not naturally qualify for, is consistent with your God-given purpose and gift, and doesn't lead you to go against Scripture.

Chapter 22

Unburden Yourself

The Word of God instructs us to lay aside the weight and the sin, which so easily ensnares us and that Jesus' yoke is easy and His burden is light.[24] Most of our lives are weighed down with activities, commitments, and affiliations.

The weight and ensnaring may be you trying to do something that God has not graced you to do. If He is not empowering us and favoring us to do the task, the job, or the ministry, then it is a weight. Relationships, partnerships, and agreements with those whom God doesn't condone are a weight. Our association with them becomes the unneeded weight that drags us down.

We have weights in life, which God destines. However, He empowers us to be victorious and successful with them. We're to take up our cross (weight) and follow Jesus. Some activities that help others may in fact be a weight that ensnares us. It's vital that we assess and discern the weights ensnaring us and disconnect, dislodge, and distance ourselves from them.

A weight may be an attitude, a behavior, or mentality which ensnares us. We need to know what's best for us. What daily routine is best for you? What activities inspire you? What environments inspire you to excellence and godly character? What geographical areas enhance, motivate, and fuel your appetite to live life to the fullest? What endeavors cause you to be full of vision and focused on a prosperous future?

> **There are specific environments, activities, and geographical areas which burden you. You need to identify them and unburden yourself.**

There are certain career paths, which cause you to advance beyond others. It is a path where the favor of God and the grace of God have opened doors and presented opportunities and promotions without you struggling or striving. This should be the path of peace for your life. A place or career should inspire you to grow, improve, succeed, give, and enjoy life.

Notice the doors the Lord has opened for you in your life and discover the path He's leading you to peace, prosperity, and progress. You can and should be all you can be in the Lord. Unburdening yourself may mean drawing a line between you and some activities, relation-ships, obligations, or locations.

Chapter 23

The Best Thing Going for You

The best thing anyone can have going for themselves is their personal relationship and fellowship with the Lord Jesus Christ. Regardless of the degree of fortune or fame one achieves, it will never come close in comparison to their relationship and fellowship with Him. He's the best thing we've got going for us. He'll always be our most valuable asset and our greatest ally.[25] He's the best benefit or benefit package offered to man.[26] He's the best thing going. He's the best bargain and the best deal. What He offers is free. He's paid for it and offers the greatest return on your investment. He doesn't ask or require of you anything you don't have or that He hasn't given you. He's the best thing going. He is the beginning and the end. Get a hold on Him. Pursue Him. He's the best thing going.

Keep Him fresh in your view. It's possible! He said He'd never leave you nor forsake you. You'll never find a better friend. You'll never find a more capable associate. Remember, He chose you before you chose Him.

CHAPTER 24

YOU HAVE HELP

When God sends you to a place or tells you to do something, you'll have help. The Holy Spirit is our Helper.[27] Conversely, if you attempt to do something He hasn't told or sent you to do, you must rely on your own efforts, strength, and ability.

If God moves you to a new job, community, or city the Holy Spirit will work with you and work things out for you. When you have help from the Helper, you may be yet to physically see all you need, but you'll have peace about it. He'll lead you to get you in the house, community, or city He desires. He'll open doors and bestow favor upon you to get you to the location of employment with the employer and coworkers He desires. You'll be guided and you'll be led. He'll get you to where you need to be and sustain you there for the duration or seasons He wants you there. He prepares your heart to be open for what He has in store. You have help. You're not in it alone. You're not working alone. The load should not be on your shoulders but on His. You have help. He works through people to help you. He'll put people in your path constantly leading, guiding, and assisting (helping) you. He uses those around you. If there is an area you don't have knowledge, He'll send someone who has the knowledge to help you. He's busy at work in your life right now, helping you. He works through others to help you and bring you success.

Help isn't on the way. Help has arrived!

Your present location is your assignment for this season. You were created to help others. Discover how you can help others and you may discover your assignment. Avail yourself to doing so and you'll experience Him helping them, using you. This is God's objective and mission on earth, to help people. All people need help all the time. The type and degree of help varies. Need for help is universal. He will help you recognize the true help that's needed, not just symptoms (what's visible). The Helper will help tune your eyes, ears, and heart to those in need of help and those ready and receptive to it. The Helper even tunes their heart to recognize you as their helper (from God). Them showing you favor may be an indication that they recognize you as someone from God to help. The prompting in you to help them may be an indication of purpose and plan of God putting you in the same path. Unknowingly, you may even speak into their lives (direction, purpose, healing, peace, and salvation).

Your genuine care for their well-being may be an indication that they're your assignment. All of this may be planned and arranged by the Holy Spirit — your Helper. He'll help you see need not apparent to the common eye. He'll help you sense and feel hurt and need, not recognizable to others. Therefore, your words have greater impact on them. Your actions have greater influence on them than the actions of others. One sentence spoken by you to them is more productive than a month's worth of conversation with others. Your words change their attitude, their direction and their outcome. All is made possible because of the Helper.

I believe God sent us the Helper because He saw beforehand, us in desperation crying help! Help! Help! We may not cry audibly, but we do cry, help! It is visible in our eyes, actions, and chaos. Always wanting to win at the expense of others may be a cry of help. Complaining in the midst of abundance may be a cry of help. Bitterness and hatefulness towards other may be a cry of help. Striving for perfection, accepting nothing less may be a cry for help. Always acting and talking as though we've never failed may be a cry for help. These things and more God saw beforehand, and gave us the Helper.

Rely on Him as your Helper. He's always available. He may not visibly help you when and how you desire. Rest assured, He's helping. Embrace Him, the Holy Spirit as your personal, always available, Helper. Take notice of the things He helps you with, consistently. Every time you put forth the effort to do, thus and so, He helps you. It's an indication of your purpose and assignment, the way and means He wants you to help others.

Chapter 25

You Are Able

The Spirit of the Lord upon you is what enables you.[28] Therefore, you are able. Since you are able and equipped with the Word of God, you enable others because God has enabled you.

The Holy Spirit is the person who enables (anoints) for ministry or any other function. Unless He anoints (enables) there is no God-given ability to do it. You can fill in the blank with any career or functions He enables people to do.

You can do it!

The Spirit of the Lord anoints men or women of God to lay hands on, prophesy, confirm, or appoint what the Holy Spirit has gifted a person to do. The Holy Sprit is the only person on earth doing the anointing. Even though the anointing flows from the head down, the Holy Spirit anoints whom He flows down to. He distributes as He wills not as we or man wills. He has to do it. A man or woman of God may tell you that you're anointed to do a specific thing. It is the Holy Spirit who anoints (enables) you. Often people try to function in capacities which they have not been enabled.

Jesus said that the Spirit of the Lord, the Holy Spirit, was upon Him.[29] It was necessary for the Holy Sprit to anoint Jesus in order for Him to do what He was destined to do. Do what the Holy Spirit has anointed you to do. It doesn't matters how bad we want to do something, what matters is whether the Holy Spirit anoints us to do it. What matters is what He (the Holy Spirit) desires us to do. It's not as I (or we) will but as He wills. We must cooperate with Him. We are workers together with Him. We must do what He (the Holy Spirit) has authorized (anointed) us to do. We must not be presumptuous. The gifts and callings of God are without repentance. If what you desire to do is not what the Holy Spirit has enabled you to do, there is something He desires to enable or has enabled you to do. He wants you to know and is leading you to do what He has anointed you to do. You will prosper as you persist faithfully in doing what He has anointed you to do. For without Him (His enabling) you can do nothing.[30] But you can do all things through His enabling which strengthens you.

CHAPTER 26

KEEP YOUR VISION ALIVE

The world needs what you have to give. No excuse or alibi you can give will suffice. There's only one you and that's all it takes. For generations the efforts of one man rather than many have made remarkable differences in people's lives. You begin in faith and God will do the rest. No more excuses.

Expand your faith. Don't limit God! Aim to reach the world — millions. Reach and serve — not impress. Expand beyond the small cove you're accustomed to. All it takes is effort. You have all the time you need. There's always time to do what you should be doing. There's never enough time to do what you shouldn't be doing.

What happened to your vision? It still exists. It'll only die if you allow it. You're the one who keeps it alive. Only you can kill your vision. No one else can kill your vision. Your vision is deep within you. It is what drives you. Keep your vision. Don't pick up another along the way. If you allow your vision to die, you begin to die. You lose your foresight, hope, ambition, and aspiration.

Nurture and nourish your vision.

Set your compass towards your vision. Envision yourself living your vision. Take a moment right now to recall your vision. Do it now, before reading further.

Now! How'd that make you feel? Did it refresh your mind? If you were able to imagine it, that means it's still alive and you just nourished it for a brief moment. Your vision needs constant nourishment—by you. No one else can nourish your vision. Stop expecting others to nourish it. All too often, you've shown others your vision expecting them to nourish it and when they don't, you're disappointed. You were disappointed because the vision is a part of you. Others want you to nourish their vision also. Every God-given vision is able to survive on it's own merit (value). True friends support each other's visions. Learn to avoid those who want you to ignore your vision. If you've tried to ignore or kill your vision and in doing so it almost killed you—keep your vision.

It's time to pursue it. Chances are, you have all the tools you need to begin. Consciously or unconsciously, you've surrounded yourself with the resources you need. Make a plan to dedicate time each week or each day to work on your vision. Working on your vision will prove therapeutic. You'll feel a sense of accomplishment.

Perhaps, your vision has been in you for several years — since you were in your teens or earlier. Perhaps you've postponed your vision. Year after year, you've told yourself that you would launch out. Don't delay any longer. Rearrange your schedule to accomplish it.

You will be more productive working on your vision than anything else you're doing or have ever done. You will do it wholeheartedly. Don't be condemned by thinking that your vision needs to be what someone else thinks it should be. Thank God for the doctors, scientists, plumbers, researchers, and construction workers who pursued their vision and we experience the benefits. We who experience the benefits of their pursuits were not there cheering them on when they began pursuing their vision.

Assess your vision to determine if it's a genuine God-given vision. What attracts you to it? If it's money, prestige, or fame it may not be God given. The occupation must draw you. You must love to do the work. It should not be laborious to you, while it may be to others. You must have a love for the work. You have the patience, endurance, and energy it takes to do it. God endowed you for it. You'll avoid meals, sleep, or recreational activities to do it. You love doing it. You gravitate toward it. You're able to do it effortlessly without thinking. You'd be surprised at how many people have worked for years even their entire lives in jobs they don't enjoy. They're making a living but they're not living.

Your vision has worked on you long enough. Now it's time for you to work on it.

CHAPTER 27

YOU'RE ALWAYS SOWING

What we sow we will reap. Therefore, why not sow to the Spirit so we can reap of the Spirit? We sow with our time, energy, thoughts, money, words, activity, and actions. Your time is one of the most valuable seeds you sow in life. Where and how you spend it is key to success and fulfillment of your God-given destiny. We are always sowing. Every moment of each day we're sowing time and energy into something. Perhaps we're dissatisfied with our harvest because it doesn't meet our expectations. Maybe where we're sowing is the cause of our less than desirable harvest.

Sow on purpose.

The Bible teaches us to sow to the Spirit. The Living Bible makes it this plain. "If he sows to please his own desires, he will surely reap a harvest of spiritual decay and death; but, if he plants the good things of the Spirit, he will reap the everlasting life which the Holy Spirit gives him. And let us not get tired of doing what is right, for after a while we will reap a harvest of blessing if we don't get discouraged and give up (Gal. 6:8-9).

Whatever we sow bountifully (in due season) we'll reap bountifully if we don't get discouraged and give up. There is a season, a time established by God, when we will experience and receive the harvest of our sowing (prayer, energy, time, or resources confession). It is vital that we sow to the Spirit with our words. Death and life are in the power of the tongue (our words). We will have what we say. I encourage you to continue to speak God's promises concerning you despite current negative circumstance. Be settled in your minds that God will do what He says. Say what He says. If His Word says it's done. You say it's done.

Allow me to give you an example of sowing to the Spirit. The time we spent writing, editing, publishing, and distributing these writings we're sowing to the Spirit. The time you're spending reading it, you're sowing to the Spirit. We will reap a harvest from the Spirit by not becoming discouraged and giving up. The time you spend praying, listening to, or thinking about the Word of God you are sowing to the Spirit.

The time you spend giving due time, attention, and care for your spouse and children, you are sowing to the Spirit. Yes, there has to be a proper balance. We should not spend every spare moment in the Bible or at church to the neglect of our loved ones. Quality time shared with your family is the best therapy for the home. Spend time listening to one another and having fun together. The same joy you display at church, on the phone with your friend, or at work needs to be shared daily with your loved ones.

Since you're always sowing, you must always have seed. Your time and energy is seed. Your thoughts and words are seeds. If they remain planted and nurtured, they'll grow. Prepare and plan to sow daily. Make it a point to sow a little daily. Spend time storing the Word of God in your mind (reading, study, and meditation). Spend time sowing the Word of God out of your mouth (confession and prayer). Spend time storm-proofing the Word of God in your life (doing). You're always sowing. Choose wisely what you sow.

CHAPTER 28

RECOGNIZE WHO READS,
NEEDS, OR HEEDS YOU

You always have those who read you, those who need you, and those who heed you.

Read you. Those who read you learn from the witness of your conduct and daily lifestyle instead of your words (your personality). They may be love ones, family, or coworkers. Your daily conduct is being observed, evaluated, and perhaps copied by those around you. It's important how you respond or react in adversity. Those who read you evaluate you through long-term observation. Often, they may not let you know they're observing and learning from you. For sure, you have such people in your life.

Need you. Those who need you draw from being around you. They may not draw or discern from your counsel or words (your presence). They may be friends, coworkers, or supervisors. Your presence makes a tremendous difference in their lives. They like having you around. Your testimony or productivity may not impress them. But your presence makes an impression upon them. God's presence in and with you helps fulfill the need in others.

Heed you. Those who heed you draw from your counsel, teaching, preaching, and correction (your proclamation). They are a congregation, a classroom, a conference, or an individual. People value what you say. It has tremendous influence upon others (either positive or negative). Others may pattern their conduct by what you say during casual conversation. Your words may be remembered and echoed in the memory of others for decades to come.

> **Who is reading you, needing you,
> or heeding you?**

You are an arrow sharpened and pointed by God to hit a specific target. Knowing your target and audience will help you remain focused, effective, and on course consistent with the grace of God towards you for the current season.

CHAPTER 29

OTHERS NEED YOU

Your wife needs "you" not just a man or a husband. She specifically needs you. Your husband needs "you" not just a woman or a wife. He specifically needs you. Your children need "you" not just a father or mother. They need their father, their mother.

Your supervisor and employer needs you not just an employee. An employee only contributes work. The person and personality of an employee contributes much more than work. Your coworkers need you not just any coworker. You must believe that you are significant in their lives for good and for God. Your supervisor depends upon you to do more than the work assigned to you. You have much more to offer than that. You were a person before you were an employee. The greatness of you as a person surpasses your greatest accomplishment as an employee. Perhaps a former employer or friend has commended you for something other than your performance. They admired you for the person you are more than the job you did or the position you possessed.

You're needed!

During relocations people may express sadness upon your departure. They miss your presence most. They missed your presence more than your position or work. Companies may pay great and offer even more to keep you. Simply because they value having you for the person you are, being of great importance and significance to them and the company. You mean a lot to others. Most of them have never told you. The few that do, tell you upon your departure.

The people you work with right now look to you for strength, comfort, peace, and counsel. Undoubtedly it is a gift from God. Don't try to be anything to anyone other than yourself. Others value having you around and being around you. It is something about you being there.

Who you are, is the most valuable thing you posses. It exceeds more than you will accomplish.

You need people too. You need your wife or husband not just a wife or a husband. You need your children not just children. You need yours.

You need those who need you. It's what keeps you alive with purpose. No matter who they are or where they are, you need those who need you. Their need for you allows the you, in you, to be. Them needing you, draws the you out of you.

CHAPTER 30

SOMEONE'S CRYING HELP!

Somebody help! This is a cry from someone in need, despair, or disappointment. It summons another person to come to the rescue. The one who cries does not discriminate about who comes to their aid. The real need is for help. The cry is intended towards those in close or closest proximity.

Are you such a person making this cry? Is there a load you have which you alone cannot sustain? If not you, there are thousands of people making this cry daily. Somebody help! They may not use the specific words "somebody help." But they may be saying it with their actions. They may be saying it through the tone of their voice. They may be saying it through their work performance. They may be saying it through drug abuse. They may be saying it through cigarettes or alcohol. They may be saying it through gestures or mannerisms. Now, can you hear them crying, "somebody help"?

Help is a word, which infers a need for unity and cooperation. Help is a word that carries substantial weight. It brings people together based on need instead of greed. It is also a gratifying experience for the one being helped and the helper. The greater the number of helpers the more force that can be exerted towards a common interest.

Help! Can anybody hear me? Help!

God created us to help and be in need of help. Understanding and applying this basic yet vital human dimension can be the key to joy and fulfillment in life. Every individual has within himself or herself something (know-how or ability) that is not meant for them but to help others. At the same time, every individual has a limitation (know-how or ability) that needs the help of someone else. Having the humility to acknowledge and allow someone to help you and having the willingness to help someone else is the key to being successful in life.

CHAPTER 31

STAY TRUE TO YOUR LINE OF WORK

There is a specific assignment you are tailor-made to perform on earth. You're the best at doing what you're supposed to do. Someone is deeply dependent upon the function you perform. If you don't do what you're destined, there's a void in someone's life or in society. God created you to bring glory to Him. When you do what He created you to do, you bring glory to Him. He has given you abilities so you can do what you were born to do. Your success and effectiveness is vital to the kingdom of God. You represent the opposite of what the devil represents.

Discover what works of the devil you're called to destroy. Jesus was manifested to destroy the works of the devil.[31] Then He said, you will do greater works.[32] He gave you power and authority to tread over the serpents, the scorpions, and over all the power of the enemy and nothing shall by any means harm you.[33] Therefore, what works are you called to destroy?

We're relying on you, to be you.

While you're busy building a work, make sure you're destroying the works of the devil. Perhaps you're called to destroy the devil's sickness and disease work, his poverty work, his depression work, his confusion work, his guilty conscious work, his lack of knowledge work, or his racism work? What work of the devil are you called to destroy?

Put your hands to doing the work you are destined to do and don't look back.[34] We're relying on you to stay true to your purpose. We're better off because of you. There are many waiting for your discovery and arrival. You are needed. You are effective. You're in great demand.

ENDNOTES

1. Genesis 18:14
2. 2 Corinthians 1:4
3. Matthew 9:37
4. Hebrews 12:2
5. Ephesians 2:20
6. Revelations 2:4-5
7. Revelations 2:4-5
8. James 1:17, Proverbs 10:22
9. Ecclesiastes 3:1
10. Jeremiah 33:3, 2 Kings 6:17
11. James 1:23
12. Amos 7:7-8
13. Philippians 4:13, Romans 8:31
14. 1 Peter 5:7
15. Ezra 4:1-5
16. Nehemiah 6:1-4
17. Ezra 4:3
18. Nehemiah 6:3
19. Psalm 107:20
20. Proverbs 4:20-22
21. 3 John 2
22. Isaiah 30:21
23. Revelations 3:8
24. Hebrews 12:1, Matthew 11:30
25. Romans 8:31
26. Psalm 103:2
27. John 14:16, 26
28. Luke 4:18
29. Luke 4:18
30. John 15:5
31. 1 John 3:8
32. John 14:12
33. Luke 10:19
34. Luke 9:62

Author Contact Information

Robert L. Smith
P. O. Box 31603
Alexandria, VA 22310

E-mail: willofgod@hotmail.com

Printed in the United States
201068BV00002B/1-105/A